Wacky Wacky Wacky Wacky PUZZLES

Brain Busting Puzzles
for Ages 6-60

Watermill Press

Rolf Heimann

First published in USA by Watermill Press

First published by Periscope Press, a division of Roland Harvey Studios, Australia.

Copyright © Rolf Heimann 1992

Designed by Debra Billson

Printed in USA

ISBN 0 8167 2615 9

10 9 8 7 6 5 4 3 2

Puzzle Preface

There is something very satisfying about solving a puzzle that has been designed to confuse you. Most of us look forward to the opportunity to prove how easily we can conquer even the most difficult problems. Sometimes we succeed, sometimes we don't. The main thing is to try.

The puzzles in this book will provide you with a thorough test of your problem-solving skills. When you finally solve the last puzzle, your brain will be in tip-top condition. Not only that, you will have had hours of fun in the process!

I wish you well on your journey through *Wacky Puzzles*.

I can't wait to get started! I'll see you inside!

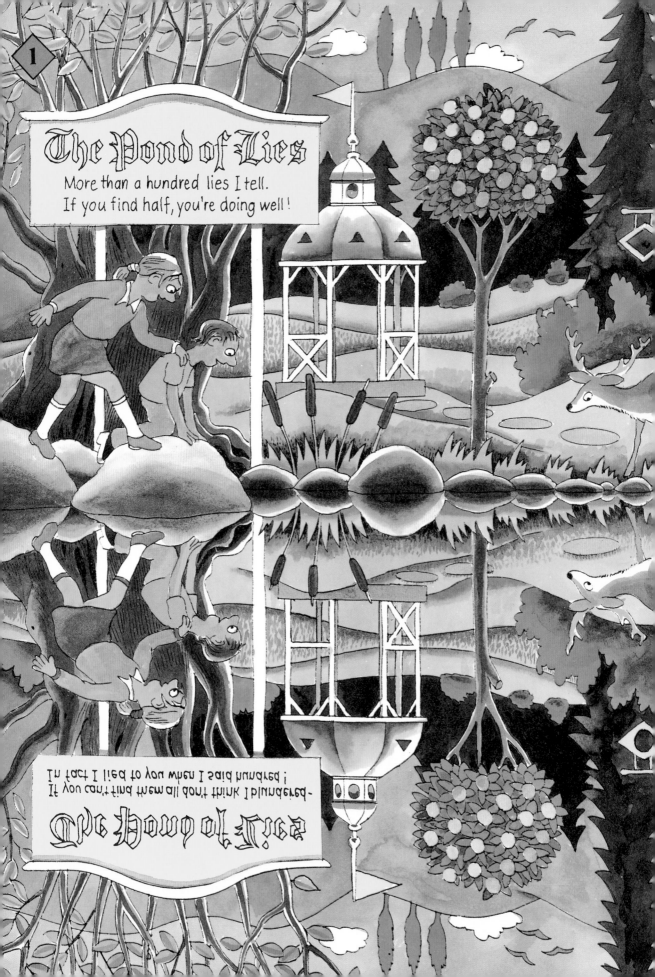

2 Step from three to thirty but move from number to number in increasing multiples of three: 3, 6, 9, etc.

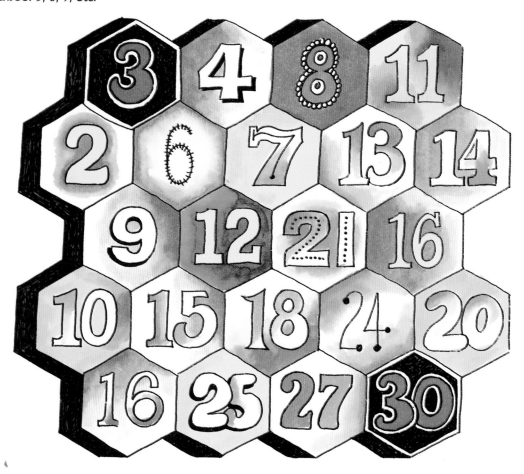

3 Nobody can fool Detective McQuick! Detective McQuick was questioning the witness to a shooting. A car had drawn up outside a restaurant and its driver had fired a dozen shots through the large plate-glass window. Luckily nobody had been hurt.

"I believe you were sitting closest to the window," said Detective McQuick to one of the customers. "What sort of car was it?"

"I saw nothing," replied the man. "I was sitting here by myself at this three-legged table and I had just bent down to put a folded paper napkin under one of the legs. It was wobbling, you see . . ." Detective McQuick interrupted him. "You are not telling the truth, sir."

How did Detective McQuick know that the man was lying?

Answers to this puzzle and the puzzle on the previous page are on page 30.

4 Transfer the lines from the top square into the grid below.

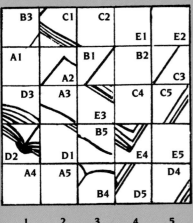

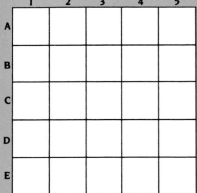

	1	2	3	4	5
A					
B					
C					
D					
E					

Answer on page 30

6

These 3 cubes are identical. All have 3 stars and 3 circles. Can you figure out whether the sides facing me show stars or circles?

Answer on page 30

7 **A** giant creature's been seen from the air!
Here are the directions to find its lair:
First look for the mountain that's crowned by a fountain,
Then follow the river that rhymes with *shiver*.
When you come to a town where most roofs are brown
Turn the page around till it's upside down.
That's where you'll find the giant mouse.
— Carefully walk beyond the last house

8

In the first year this little tree has 2 leaves.

In the second year there'll be 4 leaves.

The number doubles each year, so we'll have 8 leaves in year 3.

In the fourth year? 16 of course!

The question is: In how many years will the tree have one million leaves? In 20 years? In 1000 years? In 500,000 years?

9 Only one of the seven stars on the right looks exactly like the one below. **Which one is it?**

Answers on page 30

?

A   B   C   D   E   F   G

Tim is shipwrecked. After two days' hard rowing he finds a desert island. Luckily there is enough flotsam washed up on the beach to build a shelter. Draw a shelter that he could build.

10 Sixteen Proverbs

Two dogs and one bone will never agree,
A wreck is a beacon to ships at sea,
The early bird will get the worm,
Any harbor will do in a storm.

Don't count your chicks before they're hatched,
The ebb will take what the tide has fetched,
Seven shepherds spoil the flock,
It's too late to cast anchor when
The ship's on the rock.

Dirty water will never wash clean,
It's on finest cloth that stains will be seen,
Fruits never fall too far from their trees,
Sleep with a dog, rise with fleas.

Birds of a feather will flock together,
Vows made in a storm are gone in fine weather,
Follow the river to find the sea,
A bird in the hand beats two in the tree.

**The sixteen proverbs described above
You will find if you are clever enough!**

11 ▷ Cube confusion

Time limit: 25 seconds

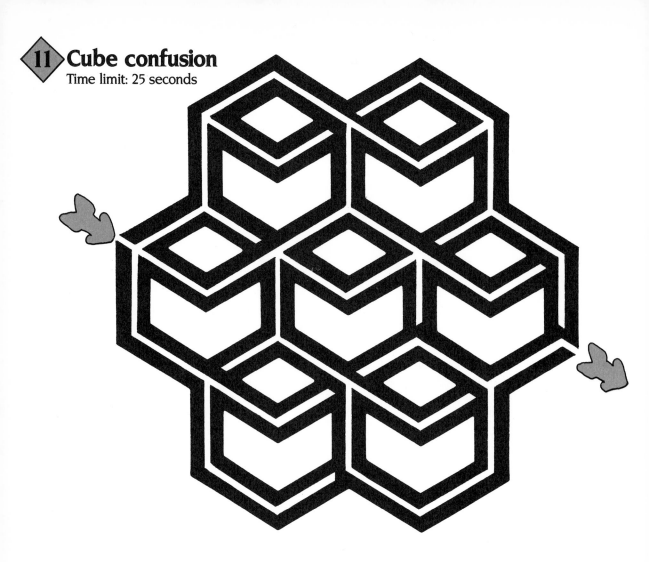

12 ▷

Find the rare four-striped yellowfish.
There is only one in existence!

Answer on page 30

14

3 Transfer the lines from the top panels onto the grids of the bottom panels.

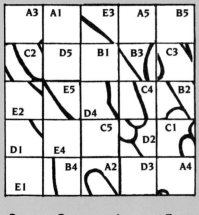

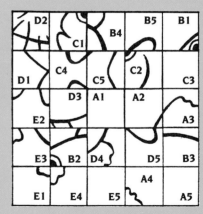

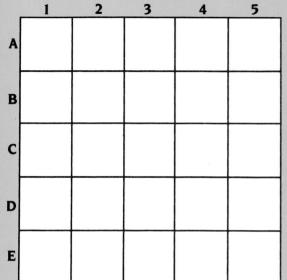

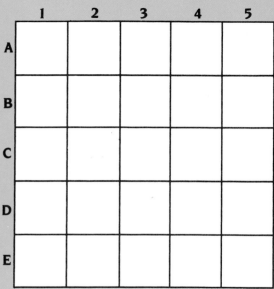

4 Two Explorers With A Problem.
After marching side by side for three weeks the two explorers were sick of each other. As soon as they had reached their destination and taken their scientific measurements, one of them said:
"If I have to spend another day with you I'll go crazy. I simply can't stand your complaining all day long."
The other replied, "And I can't stand your snoring all night long! I wouldn't stay with you if you paid me. In fact I'll start on my way back right now. Don't you start for another hour, so that there will always be 3 miles (5 kilometers) between us."
After two hours the first explorer had walked 6 miles (10 kilometers) and the second had walked 3 miles (5 kilometers).

Both had walked due south.
But the distance between them was not 3 miles (5 kilometers), but 9 miles (15 kilometers).
How was that possible?

Answers on page 30

Go to Z

15 **T**ry to make your way from A to Z without falling in the water! It shouldn't take you more than a couple of minutes.

Find the connection between the objects in the circles and make your way from top to bottom. Example: A bird can fly and so can an airplane. An airplane transports people and so does a car. A car has four wheels, and so on.

Answer on page 30

17 Eyeball to eyeball
Time limit: 15 seconds

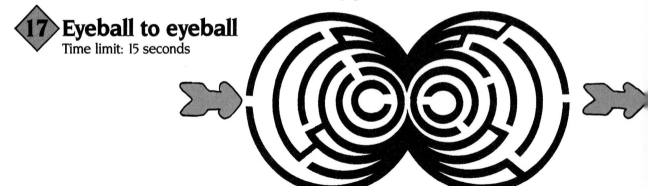

It is the astronauts' first visit to the planet Ixenplox. As they set out to explore it they are suddenly confronted by a huge monster.
Make a drawing of the monster.

19 **F**ind a connection between the items on the squares and step from the top arrows to the bottom square. Example: cat ~ dog ~ bone etc.

*Answers to this puzzle and the puzzle on the
previous page are on page 31.*

0 **T**ransfer the lines of the top panels into the grids of the bottom panels.

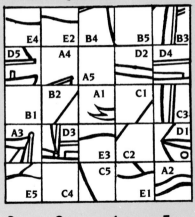

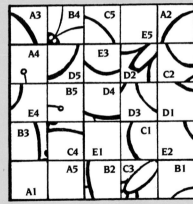

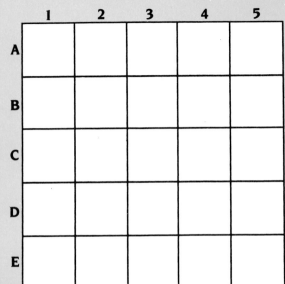

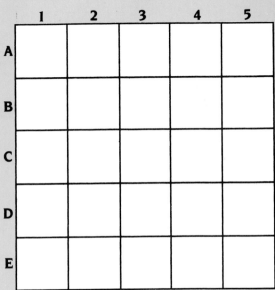

21 **S**o you think dot-to-dot drawings are too easy? Well, this one isn't.
Start with the number four and continue only in increasing multiples of four, in other words from 4 to 8 to 12. And be careful, there may be a few numbers that are only there to confuse you!

16   • 20   • 28

• 24   1 •   • 2

• 12   9 •   13 •

• 7

•8   15 •   23 •   • 32

•11   48 •   • 44   17 •

25   • 3

56   52 •   • 40   36 •

•4

Answers on page 31

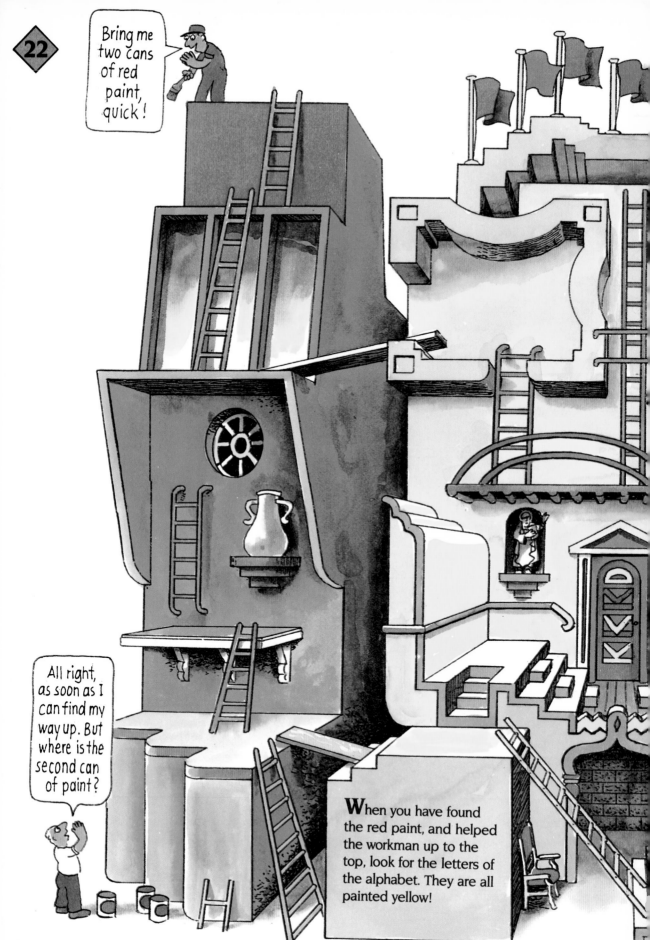

Answer on page 31

25

23 ## Steppingstones across America

23 Steppingstones across America

The arrows point to the first letter of three North American cities.

24

Fill in the missing letters. If you need help, look at a map of Australia.

25 Take the letters through the maze to find the name of a famous city in Europe.

P
R
S
A
I

The fishermen finally caught the big shark that's been terrorizing the beaches all summer. When they cut it open they found an amazing number of things it had swallowed.
Draw what the fishermen found.

26

In each row across there is a square that's the odd one out and it's from this square that you must select the letter. The word starts with O and reads from top to bottom. It's elementary . . .

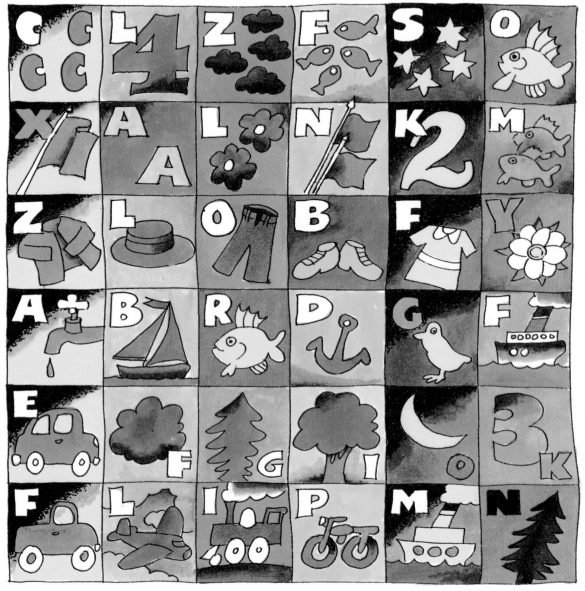

Answer on page 31

27 Parallel problem

Time limit: 45 seconds

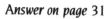

HOW OLD AM I ?
I am ten times older than my youngest son and twice as old as my oldest son. And my oldest son is 5 times older than my youngest son.

Answer on page 31

I am Ruunas, the alien. Take the letters of my name through the maze and find out where I come from!

R
U
U
N
A
S

Answer on page 31

The Answers

Here are the solutions to the more difficult puzzles.
You shouldn't need solutions to the others!

1 **Pond of lies**

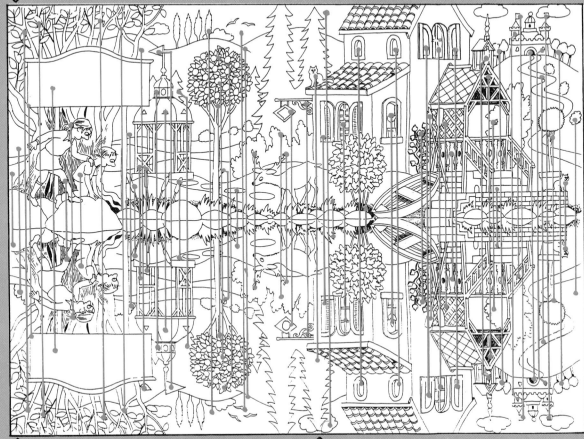

3 A three-legged table can't wobble!

4

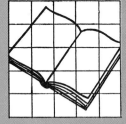

6 Cube A shows a circle, cube B shows a circle and cube C shows a star.

8 It would take 20 years for the tree to grow a million leaves (or to be exact 1,048,576 leaves).

9 Star D.

12 It's the fish at the top right.

13

14 The explorers' objective was the North Pole. They left each other going in opposite directions – and from the North Pole all paths lead due south!

16 Bird, plane, car, carriage, rattle, globe, Saturn, star, moon, night owl, rooster, pig, farmer, devil, fire, frying pan, cooked chicken, bird.

18

 20

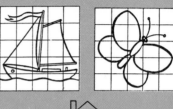

 21

 19

Starting from top left: cat, dog, bone, pirate's flag, pirate's dagger, knife, bread, butter, butterfly, two butterflies, number 2, 2 musical notes, drum.

From top right: crane, hook, fish, ship, sailing-ship, windmill, coffee grinder, chest of drawers, table, cow (4 legs), leather-bound book (both brown on yellow background), eye (to read book), glasses, musical notes, drum.

By the way, you may have found a different way through ~ that's O.K., as long as you didn't cheat!

 23 Washington, Houston, Boston.

 24 By completing the names of Australian cities from top to bottom, you can read the name of Australia's capital, CANBERRA.

 25 PARIS

 26 OXYGEN

 28 The father is 50 years old. The oldest son is 25 and the youngest is 5.

 30 URANUS

22 Letters and Ladders

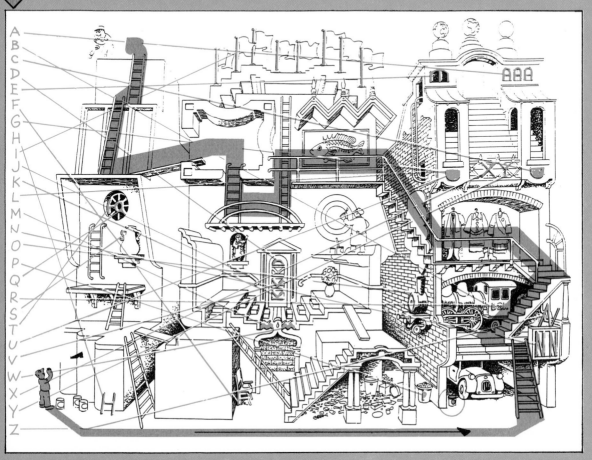